darwinii

The Comeuppance of Man

Glen Berger

with additional material by
Brett Keyser

BROADWAY PLAY PUBLISHING INC
New York
www.broadwayplaypublishing.com
info@broadwayplaypublishing.com

darwinii

© Copyright 2015 by Glen Berger

Cover graphic from Charles Darwin's *Transmutation Notebook B*
First printing March 2015
I S B N: 978-0-88145-604-2
Book design: Marie Donovan
Page make-up: Adobe Indesign
Typeface: Palatino
Printed and bound in the U S A

DARWINII: THE COMEUPPANCE OF MAN, was commissioned by the American Philosophical Society (A P S) Museum in Philadelphia. The first performance was on 16 October 2009. The cast was:

CRISTÓBAL .... Brett Keyser

Voiceover .... Laylage Courie

CHARACTERS & SETTING

CRISTÓBAL

Setting: Here

Time: Now

Note on Set: The conceit is that space has been rented by the Federal Bureau of Prisons so that our man can deliver his Apology. Therefore, the set can appear to be dressed quite plainly, at first. As the narrative continues, any props, set, and lighting shifts can be introduced unobtrusively, with CRISTÓBAL *utilizing whatever is at hand to suggest, say, a rifle as he recounts his time on the Falklands. He'll also have concealed a cache of "wares" that he reveals at the appropriate time.*

(First, the Curtain Speech [**see Appendix B**]. Then, a wild-eyed man in bright orange prison jumpsuit appears. He is wearing handcuffs, but before the end of the second page, he has revealed a key [secreted in his mouth? Disguised as an earring?] that he employs to get his cuffs off. Over the course of the show he shall shed his prison clothes, to reveal more flamboyant, idiosyncratic fashion, perhaps inspired by gaucho-wear. He has a South American accent—somewhat Argentine but mostly untraceable AND, he has blue eyes.)

CRISTÓBAL: I am here to apologize.

I am going to apologize.

I am not going to apologize *yet* because I don't see why I have to apologize, there is no REASON I have to apologize, I will apologize.

In time.

I am here…to explain. But most of all I am here to offer you special prices on special items, do not go away now or you will be sorry, you must stay here, you really must, because they locked the door, but look, it's cool, you're with me… Look, I am here because the system, the judges the crooked, the system the security system it was off I disconnected, I am here because I assumed the *yellow* wire, not the—who the hell makes the red wire the!— I am here because I've been sentenced to Three Thousand Hours of community service!

Which, if you ask me…is a bit excessive.

I am here because I am expected to recount then
recant my deeds, scare straight any wayward youth,
ask forgiveness, publicly, from the institutions I have
wronged, yes to apologize, and they'll be back for me
in an hour, but until then I am here, *here, not* in jail,
no!, because I am clever because I am Cristóbal, *because
I am Cristóbal I am not going away*, I am here *because I
survive....*

(He takes a moment to let that sink in)

Eh?

(Pause)

I Survive. Why are *you* here? Hanh? *(Singling out
an audience member)*Yes, I am talking to you, but do
not answer, I know the answer. *You* survive. Not as
Cristóbal because I am Cristóbal, that is my niche,
(Threatening) and nobody fills my niche but me, you
understand, do not get up in my niche. "Or What?"
Hm? Hanh? You want to know your options? "or
what"?

*(He wheels around, whipping out a knife as he does, and
continues to brandish it, etc. as—)*

I protect it. My *niche.* You did not know I possessed
this little friend. *Mi cuchillo.* Fwoosh fwoosh. There is
many creature that defend itself with a sharp thing.
I am one. Hedgehog, *echidna,* I am rose, *(Brandishing
knife) this is my thorn.*

Are you impressed with me yet? You will be. And then
you will take out your wallets. Until then—take me in.
Behold. This is my body. You may picture me naked if
you like. I was born with this body. This and nothing
else. Not even this. I had to grow my own teeth.
Twice! And I had to make this *cuchillo. (Wielding knife)*
Perhaps this is my only defense. *(He throws the knife on
a table)* You may take me on now if you have the need.

Anyone? No? You are wise. Because *(Whipping out another knife)* THIS little blade I also possess. Did you see how I whipped it out? *(He demonstrates again, as).* My reflexes are absurd! *(He throws the knife from hand to hand as—)* And I am ambidextrous! *(Tangos)* I was born nimble with natural grace and I exploit these skills to arouse the ladies. English I speak like a native, you did not know I am not American. Because I am a better mimic than a parrot, and it is useful for there are times I must blend in. You know the katydid with wings like dead brown leaves? I am like that. But better. *(He waggles the knife in his hand)* I can waggle a knife this fast. I am a blur with a blade, as I am happy to demonstrate to any who will jump me. *(Threateningly)* Eh!? Eh?! *(Calming)* Okay. We're cool.

Now let's be clear.

The penal system wants to be enlightened. Good for them. So I do three months on the inside and three thousand hours out here—they drop me off, they pick me up, it's okay. But. I had to agree to certain things. Like speaking with cuffs on. *(dismissively)* Pfff. And I had to assure the authorities I won't try exploiting this Apology for financial gain. So let's be clear—I don't want any money from you.

(He sets down his hat upside-down as—)

All I'm doing is taking off my hat. Because my head is hot. Just putting it down. If I pick up my hat and, hell, find *money* in it, well…these things happen and no one's the wiser and I'm just saying is all. And if I point out times to avail yourself of miraculous bargains on offer this evening, this will be a favor to *you*, I do not stand to profit. Much.

Okay. I am ready for the apology.

(He unfolds a sheet of paper.)

"I am Cristóbal and I—"

—what's amusing is—they don't know the half of it!—
the things I did—if they knew all of it... *(More solemn)*
No, who knows what they would have done if they
had heard about...*about Janice*—but no, I just have to
read this little piece of, okay—

(Reads—)

"I am Cristóbal, and I was apprehended whilst
desecrating a sacred monument and was thereafter
discovered to have stolen rare books and other
materials pertaining to the naturalist Charles Robert
Darwin." I committed this to memory. Does it look
like I am reading? For I am not. I don't know how to
read. Okay? I don't know how to read. But I get by.
Now where was I? *(resumes "reading")* "Charles Robert
Darwin. I pilfered these priceless books and documents
from the following institutions and repositories:
the Newberry Library, the Pierpont Morgan, the
Biblioteque Nationale, the American Philosophical
Society in Philadelph"— *(Interrupting himself)* okay,
you know what? I can't apologize yet because this is...I
can't endorse—because Charles Darwin...—do you
know what I have done for that man!? *(Getting worked
up—)* This is a farce! They need to grow up a little! Eh?!
Try growing up where I grew up without smacking
into Darwin!—Darwin Bay, Darwin Street, Darwin
Park, Darwin—what the hell!—Bus Station! I grew up
in Ushuaia.

(Calming—)

That's Tierra del Fuego. Argentina. I almost drowned
in Beagle Channel. Seven years old. That's the age
of reason. Or so say the catholics. So I'm confirmed,
and *mi Viejo*—my father—he's already pfffft—*gaucho*
knife fight nonsense—but my great grandmother?
Mi bisabuela? She gives me a bible. I'm at the age of

reason, so I get a bible. *(Holds up an old bible) This* bible, the family bible, I couldn't read it. I still can't read it. *(Picking up paper with apology on it)* Remember this apology? *(Waves it in front of his face)* Useless. I would use it to wipe my bottom. If it were softer. BUT! This bible changed my life. Not any bible, *this* bible, and I will tell you how. Not now. I am telling you how I was taken out in a pleasure boat when I am seven cause confirmation is a big bloody deal, and mi bisabuela had just read to me about that boat in the bible, Noah's boat, so I'm thinking about animals on a boat. I didn't know then that the number of species that have been on this planet? One hundred billion.

Yeah. On a boat.

Well I don't know—maybe if you stack the moss, get a big bucket for the bacteria, sure, okay, but like I said, I didn't know this when I was seven, and suddenly a SWELL and now I'm drowning in a beagle channel I always thought was named after a dog. But No, it's flipping Darwin again!—The H M S *Beagle*—the ship that carried young-man Darwin and opened his eyes. This wide. Carried him to my homeland. Twice. Darwin—went around the world but almost drowned in Beagle Channel. 1832. Now it was *my* turn to almost drown. And it was my mother's turn to drown.

(Pause)

Just…drown.

(Beat, intensely—)

Do not think that natural selection has forged you into anything more than a square of toilet paper—one square! Now sop up a spill as big as the universe. You will lose…you will drown…you will disintegrate…

(Makes a whooshing sound, of disintegration and silencing of mother)…Estúpido. But okay. That's fine. That's fine.

I move on. You see? Adapt, you have to, she dies, then
Perón dies, smart people die or they're disappeared,
like Uncle Luis with the pamphlets, sometimes you
have to be smart and not be so smart, no? School?
Who needs it, forget it, orphan need money, Darwin
the ticket, down to the market, get a table, sell Darwin
tchotchkes to the tourists, get the Tchotchke Man next
to me to explain me some Darwin for ideas.

*(The Tchotchke Man has a foreign accent—American?
Australian?)*

"On the Origin of Species."

Fine.

"First edition."

Like I care. Just give me something I can use.
Something to make me some money cause I'm hungry.

"How about something on the struggle for survival?"

I'm nodding.

"Imagine a log."

Okay.

*"The log is a place. And the wedges hammered in?
The iron wedges? Those are these species living in the
place. And the log is covered with these iron wedges,
so many wedges that any new wedge will send an old
wedge flying. You dig? A new better-shaped wedge
can knock the old wedge out."*

Okay. I don't get it but Okay. I get a log. It's salame.
Good salame in Ushuaia. And if you got big pants,
easy to steal. So I steal salame—hey, I'm not gonna
sell an actual log— it's a tchotchke!, it has to be small!,
cheese, those are the wedges. Little cuts in the log,
wedge in the cheese, took me forever, Darwin con
Queso. Veinte pesos!, tourists are buying like crazy!
You know why? Cause they like Darwin!

(Beat, then reveals—)

Naahhh—cause they like *salame*! Claro. And I'm knocking the boludo next to me out of business and of course I am-—'cause even when I'm ten I'm whip-smart and what was his tchotchke anyway? What is that?

"Cologne."

With a picture of old man Darwin on the bottle. *(Sniffs)* Okay that smells foul.

"It's De Scent of Man."

Hanh?

"You wouldn't get it. The English'll get it. De Scent of Man."

What the hell?

"Darwin had a book, De Scent of Man. See?"

A book about cologne?

"Nah. Sex."

Nice.

"Sexual selection and Descent with Modification." He reads me 'Sexual selection has the delightful effect of generating weapons, ornaments, songs, and colors, especially on male animals.'"

Uh huh. So why your cologne smell like old fish?

"Cause it's like what Darwin said—we still have gills."

Get off.

"We do! Vestiges of our fishy history!"

So is that why I got webbed feet? Cause we were also once ducks?

"What?"

I got webbed feet! Skin between the toes!

"Can I see?"

No! Go to hell! *(To audience)* I had enough of this guy.
I broke his nose. Well, he broke mine, same difference,
told me I was getting up in his niche and to get the hell
out of the Darwin Tchochke Business.

I didn't care. I took tourists round the nuevo Parque
Nacional Tierra Del Fuego instead. Out where the old
boy used to tramp in 1832 when he was here. Hey, if
Mister Longbeard is where the money is, then that's
where I'm gonna be, okay?, it isn't parasitic it isn't
parasitic it isn't parasitic.

(Beat)

It's commensal. One species benefits, the other—
unaffected. Darwin—he's not affected. He's the big
shark, and I'm the little remora with my little sucker,
I hitch a ride it's good it's *bon está bien*, it's tit for tat.
That's symbiotic. Or at least, you know, tit. That's
commensal. How do I know all this if I can't even read
the label on my underpants? Her name is Janice, I'll get
to her.

(Beat, face grows dark)

Janice.

(Beat, more solemn)

If there's any apologizing to be done, it should be to
you dear one, to you…. But it's too late for that…

(Shakes it off—)

So I'm giving tours, unauthorized, but who cares,
big park, plenty of room. Or so you'd think. But tour
guides, they're territorial—this Park one big salame
and I'm a wedge of chubut cheese about to get wedged
out?! No way, that's not happening to me—I need
to specialize and fast, so think—these tourists—why
are they here? What do they want? *(lightbulb, [snaps*

finger]) The Charles Darwin Experience! Dash down
to the library, get out some Darwin—for the pictures,
right?—okay, big beard, bald—I can't do that, but hold
on—that was later! When he was down here with the
Beagle, he was twenty-three!, just a little older than
me!, so get some sideburns brother! No time to grow
them, paste them on!, nick a waistcoat, and now look
at me, I *am* Charles Darwin!, right this way ladies and
gentlemen watch your step as I discover new flora and
fauna right in front of you!

And I'm making it all up, cause I'm fifteen and I don't
know jack, but like I said, I'm a master mimic, so
bango, you should have seen my tips, I was thriving!
Except my Darwin? Spawns all these other Darwins!
You can't throw a rock now without hitting a Darwin!
Every tour guide's got the sideburns, the waistcoat,
tramping through the lenga trees with bad English
accents and where are my tips!? No more leg-up!
Everything's getting divvied up equally, except for a
one centimo advantage not to me, but to *Paolo* cause
he's actually, you know, read the books. *Voyage of the
Beagle* and all that. So I'm wedged out and I'm back on
the streets of Ushuaia, and that is no fun.

And this pal Osvaldo says to me, "you want free
food?" Yeah. "Free bunk?" Yeah. "Join the army, they
take anyone."

And yeah, why not—cause I'm dying out here. So I lie
about my age and they don't even notice my webbed
feet. "Okay, what are your skills?" My skills? I can
speak English like an American. Cause I'm a master
mimic. Like a parrot. And I was born nimble with
natural grace and *(As if about to start his spiel—)* Picture
Me Naked, and yeah they took me in. Told me my
specialty would be Alarm Systems. Hanh? "The whole
compound needs an upgrade, so you can apprentice—
You can't read worth jack but you just need to

remember the colors of the wires, you can do that, can't
you?" I *can* do that! So this was my new niche, and as
niches go, it's good, it's *bon está bien*, I'm splicing wires
and banking paychecks down in Tierra del Fuego and
what—like we're going to go to war? With Ecuador?
Nah, I'm set.

And then one day this sergeant from "A" Company
says, "No. Not Ecuador. Englaterra." Hanh? "Get your
boots on, Great Britain's getting up in our niche." *Hijos
de putos.*

And then he says, "Darwin is on fire." He's *what*?
"Darwin!" Who the hell sets a dead guy on fire?! But
it's not Darwin, it's *Darwin*, the capital of Las Malvinas,
so Yeah, now I gotta go defend Darwin! Look at
history, it's what people do—go be Darwin's bulldog,
cause people can't help but lob bombs at the guy, it's
exhausting.

So we're heading out to Las Malvinas—the Falkland
Islands—to make a stand near Darwin on Darwin
Ridge, right by Darwin School, which overlooked
Darwin Bay, and it didn't take a genius to figure out
Charles Darwin visited the Falklands too. Made notes
about the Falkland Island Fox. Said the whole species
would kick it in thirty years cause the Falkland Island
Fox was naïve and trusting so you could lure it with
a piece of meat in this hand and then stab it with this
hand, and he was right! By Nineteen Hundred, pfffft!
No more fox. Well that was never NEVER gonna
happen to me, I'm not naïve!, but I can't escape, cause
—what the hell—it's an island! —so I gotta go back and
shells are pounding and we're hunkered down and it's
night and we're in trouble. And it's bad. It's bad and
loud, and skin's dripping off the arm of Osvaldo, and
I'm in a little hole on a little island and I can't see until
something explodes, and then I don't *want* to see, just
stay in your foxhole and try not to go extinct, you're

alone but who cares if you're alone, you're alone, so
nobody cares. So I get out mi bisabuela's bible. To
pray? Nah. Give me a break—I keep something in it.
(He holds up a lock of hair) A lock of hair. From my
mother. *Mi vieja.* We're mammals. Mammals have *hair.*
It keeps us warm. I was a little warmer in that foxhole,
clutching this lock…it was like clutching a thread to
the past. *My* past. And speaking of my past—check it
out —In the back of the bible, there is a tree someone
in my family drew. A family tree. And see? *(Holds up
bible) Mi bisabuela* put me on this twig on top—drew me
in when I was seven. I look nice, I look good up there,
like a monkey or something. So I'm in this foxhole,
and wondering if I'll ever get a chance to add some
twigs of my own to this tree, when I notice a lump in
the binding I never noticed before, and I take out my
army-issued *cuchillo* cause any excuse to take out a
cuchillo, and pfffft, I gut it like a fish, and out plops…
destiny.

*(Holds up a piece of paper—it is ripped and incomplete.
It has a diagram [incomplete at the rip] of branching,
resembling the tree of life diagram made by Darwin in
Transmutation Notebook B)*

It's a piece of paper. I can't really see cause it's dark
and there's mud and blood but it looks like another
family tree someone's drawn. But no pictures no
names. *(Blasé)* I've seen it before. This tree, this
handwriting, it's no big deal, I've seen it before, I just
can't remember where. *(Then less blasé) No, I remember
where.*

On that book! In the Ushuaia Library! The book I
got, to get a bead on how I needed to make Darwin's
sideburns! This was the picture on the cover! But what
the hell?! Why was this on that book?! Maybe I was
just delirious, going mad, but one thing was sure—I

had to get off this island! And now it's dawn and we're storming down Darwin Hill by Darwin School toward Darwin Bay, and Ernesto is hit in the groin and he's gone, but my groin is good, it's *bon está bien*, and the next day Piaggi surrenders us all and I don't care, I'm alive.

(Beat)

I'm alive.

Back on the mainland, I go AWOL—I'm not sticking around that scene, are you kidding me. No, I disappear, I blend in, and better than any katydid ever did, like this— *(He poses)* —right? You can barely see me.

So now I'm on a mission. I slip down to the Ushuaia Library and I find the book, I find the picture, but what *is* the picture?, like suddenly I can read? *(Shaking head)* this is the brain I'll always have. But I wasn't done yet cause on the back of the book *(Scutinizing—)* was a picture of Darwin as a Lady, he was dressing as a lady, or no it was just a lady, some lady, I guess she wrote the book, bright blue eyes, looked smart, looked really...she...I liked how she smiled....

And then what should have taken me three minutes took me nine years. I am serious people. Took me nine years to find out the library also has something called "books on tape." Apparently there are signs all over the library that tout it. All over. I imagine the blind, the illiterate, would find these signs very helpful if we could, you know, read them! Okay. I move on. Nine years after I see the picture of the smiling lady, I find the book-on-tape which has on the back the same picture of the same lady so I know we're good, hit the button.

(He plays the tape.)

BOOK-ON-TAPE ANNOUNCER: Orchard Press Audio Books presents…*The Tree of Life: The Roots of Darwin's Greatest Discovery*. By Janice Greene. Read by the author.

(A little introductory music on the tape as—)

CRISTÓBAL: Janice. Her name was Janice…

JANICE: *(On tape)* Devoting one's life to the study of Charles Darwin was not exactly *encouraged* where I grew up…. Although the mountains of Southern Appalachia were formed over four hundred million years ago, my ma and pa and almost all the other folks in the Tennessee town of my youth figured those hills couldn't be much over six thousand years old because the Bible suggested as much…

(As JANICE *continues to speak, **see B-roll below,* CRISTÓBAL *says—)*

CRISTÓBAL: And her voice was milk, was silk—that voice, that soul, this was a woman who *knew*, I'm telling you she turned me on, cause I could tell—she had the *answers*, and so long as she was speaking, I wasn't alone, I wasn't alone.

JANICE: In fact, the town of Dayton was just down the road—Dayton, where in 1925 a young High School football coach subbing for the Principal in Science Class, taught evolution to young impressionable minds and wound up in court. And of course everyone knew it wasn't just John Scopes who was on trial, but that instrument of the devil himself—Charles Robert Darwin.

CRISTÓBAL: So with her words pouring into my ear, I waited to hear about the little picture on the front of her book—

(By this point, we have faded down JANICE *and faded up again on a later section—)*

JANICE: *(On cassette)* Which brings us to the illustration found at the front of this book. He couldn't draw. He admitted as much. The little sketch he made in Transmutation Notebook B resembles a bladderwort as much as a tree, an aquatic plant floating on the sea, spreading not upwards but *outwards*—and that, *that* was the radical revelation, the call-it-proto-communist declaration our strangely insecure brain cells still resist acknowledging—*all life is equal*—there is no advancement, no higher, no lower, hold this book not vertically but horizontally to understand Darwin's revolutionary doodle...

(As increasingly stirring music underscores, JANICE *continues low underneath* CRISTÓBAL'*s speech—**see B-roll below)*

CRISTÓBAL: I was right. It *was* a family tree. Only the family is something called Life. *(Beat)* It's a sketch for the Tree of Life—there was already a tree of life in that bible— *Mi bisabuela* would read to me about it but that was just some tree that was supposed to give you immortality if you ate its fruit or rubbed up against it, the bible isn't clear, but *this*. This was an explanation, a picture, of how all living things, all one hundred yes *billion* types of living things, are connected, are

JANICE: Branches beget branches Embryophytes to Bryophytes to Spermatophytes spawning Dicots, Monocots, Eudicots— orchids, lilies, grasses, poppies, palms, magnolias no more, no less advanced, than dinoflagellates, radiolarians, the diatoms and kelps and molds and jellies; sponges, corals, humans and minnows, hagfish, whales, rats, dinosauria, mammalia, reptilia, to the Holothurians "Hosanna" related, are interrelated, and if I can still be a monkey at the top, then sign me up for a new brain cause mine just got blasted into the night sky where it exploded into tiny fizzy stars.

cue the cucumber see cucumber sea cucumber, coelacanths, they have pouches, they lay eggs, the tail is visible, they have no tail, *(Fading up)* …they're star-like they're spiny, a single hole, an odd-toed ungulate, they're curl-footed, ten-footed, devour flesh and have wings in a sheath, all life one Life, all life one Life, one tree, come meet the family, the radial symmetry of the anenome, all life one Life, all life one Life…

CRISTÓBAL: So okay. I cannot read, and that has only sharpened my visual acuity. I can see a hawk before a hawk can see *me*. I can recognize in the swirl and curl of smoke something poetic which I will think of later if you remind me. So from the little jots on my piece of paper, and the little jots on the cover of the book of Miss Greene, I can tell you with the confidence of a Man With No Shirt Hauling Rope that the handwriting? Is the same.

(To audience) Now Sit up Straight—I'm not saying this twice. The picture on the book came from a sketch that was sketched in Transmutation Notebook B, after Darwin returned to England in 1837. So how did a similar version wind up in my great grandmother's bible?

I remember her telling me she got the bible from her *abuela*, who would read it aloud to *her* illiterate mother. Her illiterate mother who was—look at the family tree!—a young woman when the Beagle made land again in 1834. You see? She ripped a page of Darwin's notebook when he wasn't looking, and he had to draw it again when he got home. Why'd she do it? Who the hell knows. And you know what? It's completely far-fetched. So forget it, I forgot it. Stupid idea. But so long as I had this book-on-tape, I figured I'd give the whole thing a listen. And another listen, and another, and—

Now look—Pop was a *gaucho*. He had Spanish blood, he had Patagonian blood, who knew what the hell blood he had. Mother, on the other hand, was full-blooded Fuegian. One of the last. Cause Fuegians were wiped out years ago by smallpox, brought to South America by Europeans immune to smallpox cause years of Europeans *dying* of smallpox meant those in Europe still standing had a gene which ensured they *wouldn't* die of smallpox. But for those of you who *don't* believe in natural selection, there's another explanation—it involves a magical squirrel, on a rampage. So take your pick.

I will start again. I want to be clear about this. Because there are those who believe I owe Martin Fierro an apology. Yes, I strangled him. Not to death, no—I was pulled off the devil before I could, but I tell you why I did it—he was swinging a stick in the air and it nearly poked my eye out and these eyes….

…these eyes are my treasures. *These eyes—blue like the blue ice of Patagonian glaciers but bluer—these eyes will redeem me.* Any man tries to prise these eyes out of me, I will gut him, skin him, treat the skin with preserving chemicals, stuff the skin, mount it on a handsome base of coihue—it's a nice hardwood—I'll stain it, and I will sell this mounted man for fifty pesos, which is what I charge for any Patagonian otter.

Now pay close attention. *Closer. (Singling out one—)*
You—closer. There was a time when all the world had
brown eyes. And then, like yesterday, practically, a
baby near the Black Sea was born. 7000 years ago. Her
eyes? Blue . Her name was Matilda. It wasn't, but I
say it was, and I have at least two knives so her name
was Matilda, and she was guapísima—five foot two,
eyes of blue, okay a mutant, cause she's new, but she
found a mate and I want to be very clear about this.
Three thousand years *before* Matilida, Fuegians settled
in Fuego, and that means *not a scrap of blue is in the
Fuegian eye.* Now genetics ain't my bag but thanks to
Janice I know more than Darwin, so I dig that both
parents need blue to get the blue to you, *(Pointing to his
eyes)* so these eyes? *(To his unseen mother)* These eyes
mean, *mi madre*, that *you* were not full-blooded. Some
undocumented blood is rushing through our veins—
some blue-eyed devil bedeviling our D N A and if
that's so—I had listened to *The Tree of Life* by Janice
Greene ten twenty times. Even so, I played it again, just
on a whim. *(He hits the button on the tape recorder)*

JANICE: *(On tape)* One hundred billion species. Tens,
hundreds, or thousands of millions of individuals
comprising each of these one hundred billion species—
to focus on only one of these individuals seems almost
perverse but such is life. The colored speck of the
cosmic kaleidoscope named Charles Robert Darwin
first appeared in Shrewsbury England, in February
1809, the blue-eyed second son of a prosperous medical
doctor, Robert—

CRISTÓBAL: *(Interjecting at "blue-eyed")* What the hell?!

*(*CRISTÓBAL *rewinds—)*

JANICE: —in February 1809, the blue-eyed second son
of a prosperous—

CRISTÓBAL: *(Interjecting at "blue-eyed")* Hijo de puto!

(CRISTÓBAL *rewinds—)*

JANICE: *...the blue eyed—*

CRISTÓBAL: Yes....!

(CRISTÓBAL *rewinds—)*

JANICE: *—blue eyed—*

CRISTÓBAL: *Yes...!*

(Music as CRISTÓBAL *throws open his arms wide—)*

CRISTÓBAL: Behold and Wonder, Ye People. Behold
Charles R Darwin's GREAT GREAT GREAT GREAT
GRAND BASTARD!

(Here, CRISTÓBAL *tangos as* JANICE *reads—)*

JANICE: Life dances with itself—who leads?, who
follows?—it's all one and ever-shifting in a tango
of desire and survival, til extinction—the tap on the
shoulder—sends a new dancer dipping swaying
lunging stamping and all toward nowhere in
particular, no reason, no end, never ending, coalescing
in the pivot slice searing grace of *you* Cristóbal, *you*
who can hear my unspoken words assure you that you
do not dance alone, loss does not sever links, no my
love, *know,* my love, that you are lashed to Life itself
for Life is *you* and, as Our Man once wrote, *"there is
grandeur in this view."*

(Meanwhile, CRISTÓBAL *has gotten out a display of the
wares he will be selling, and continues to Tango as—)*

CRISTÓBAL: Okay so *Now.* This is the time, do not
delay. I have many quality products on display,
please, get out your pocketbooks, I have...*On the
Origin of the Species!,* signed by an actual descendent
of the great man—me. I have, wrapped in tissue, hair!,
plucked from a bona fide descendent of the father
of Evolution—Me! *(Holding up a container—)* This,
gentlemen, is Grade A saliva, extracted from a bona

fide member of *darwinii*—a great conversation piece.
AND for a very reasonable price— *(Holding up a pipette
of semen)* —a pipette containing hundreds of millions
of micro-organisms carrying genetic treasure of great
historical worth. Ladies, this is a rare opportunity
to breed with the progeny of undisputed genius.
Curiosity, Attentiveness, Perseverance—these are just
some of the qualities that made Charles Darwin the
greatest lover since Casanova. These traits could very
well be genetic, and don't your progeny deserve the
best? And for tonight only, two-for-one—any book
plus any pipette, one low price!

(Ad-libbed to end of music:)

Please, form an orderly line. There is no need to push,
there is plenty for all and I assure you there is more
where this came from. No one will leave this evening
disappointed. So, who will be first to take home a piece
of history?

Okay. I see you need more proof. That's cool. In
my heart I knew instantly it was true, but like good
scientists we must be walloped with proof. Like my
great great great great grandfather with *his* theory, I
would amass enough evidence to smother a horse!—
like Charles, who spent twenty years crouching in the
shadows of Down House, waiting—waiting to knife
the scientific establishment in its plump gut—I too
would crouch…then jump the world, and demand it
hands over its pocketbook!

So first things first. Janice mentions that he wrote a
book describing his time on and off that boat. Okay, so
that's all I needed, I thought. So through great effort,
I acquired the book-on-tape. *The Voyage of the Beagle*.
And halfway through, Darwin describes the day in
December, a little after noon, when he entered the
Bay of Good Success. He had arrived at my home! *(He*

*presses the button on tape recorder. We hear sound of canoes
in the water—)*

VOYAGE OF THE BEAGLE BOOK-ON-TAPE NARRATOR:
(Quoting from Voyage of the Beagle*)* "…We pulled
alongside a canoe with six Fuegians. These were the
most abject and miserable creatures I anywhere beheld.
These poor wretches were stunted in their growth,
their hideous faces bedaubed with white paint, their
skins filthy and greasy, their hair entangled, their
voices discordant, and their gestures violent. One can
hardly make one's self believe that they are fellow-
creatures. I believe, in this extreme part of South
America, man exists in a lower state of improvement
than in any other part of the world…"

CRISTÓBAL: *(Somewhat devastated)* "Hideous faces"?
"Hard to believe they're fellow creatures"? My
ancestors—that's who he's talking about! And he
thinks they're no better than animals? Well to hell
with him. That's what I thought. To hell with Charles
I'm-So-Important-Cause-I'm-From-Europe Darwin.
And then I got to thinking. He laid it on a bit thick,
dontcha think? I mean—these are my kin! Okay maybe
they weren't up on the latest way to hold a fork, but
one look in the mirror tells me—they were looking
just fine. And you're telling me you're a man, a full-
blooded man, a young man, on a ship without so much
as the captain's grandma for feminine company, and
you're telling me you find the topless ladies of del
Fuego *hideous*? Ho ho—nice try Mister Darwin, but
this fish ain't biting. *On the contrary*, I get to thinking…
My blood is his blood and after two weeks, *I'm* ready
to bed down with an otter, and we're talking about a
man who fathered ten children as soon as he got back
to England! And that's just with his wife! We're talking
about a man who understood like no man before him
reproductive strategy. We're talking about a man who

traveled all over the world in the Beagle describing the
hideous features of Australian ladies, Brazilian ladies,
ladies in New Zealand, Peru, Tahiti, the male cod
inseminates ten thousand eggs, *how about you, Mister
Darwin?* And then I could have hit myself—of course!

(He holds up a notebook.)

This. The ladies here perhaps do not recognize what
this is, but the gentlemen do, yes, you are nodding
your heads. For every man possesses one of these. Am
I right? A List of Sexual Conquests. *(Flipping through
it, demonstrating)* This is mine and it is almost filled.
Almost. Not with names of course...*but portraits.* I
knew their names, I just didn't know how to write
them down. And yes, auténtico, every page! Except
maybe some at the beginning—it is customary to get
a running start in one's Sexual Conquest notebook.
Generally, extrapolating from my own experience—
whenever men get together, they compare notebooks.
That is how it is. How it was, how it is, and how it
ever shall be. And with blessed clarity my task became
clear. And I would have to act fast, because no doubt
Darwin left bastards all over the globe, and they'll be
laying their claims, and I'm going to have to fight them
off—if any bastard's going to be making money off of
Charles Darwin, it's *this* Bastard! So my plan is simple.
My plan is elegant. After marrying, surely he hid it
but he did not destroy it—*I must get ahold of Darwin's
Notebook of Sexual Conquests.* The name at the bottom of
this bible will be on that list of his, and then I'll have it.
I'll have my proof!

Now any scholar worth their salt would know which
museum, which archives, this notebook of Darwin's
was residing in. But there was only one scholar for me.
In a conference in Cleveland, there would be the fusing
of two unplumbable souls—souls intent on mining the

legacy of Charles Darwin for personal financial gain—
my soul, and the soul…of Janice Greene!

I recorded her speech, so I could review it at my
leisure…

(We hear JANICE *on the cassette, at what sounds like a
conference hall)*

JANICE: *(On tape)*
It is indeed a great honor to
be recognized by my peers
for throwing perhaps a
little more light on the   CRISTÓBAL:
ideas of this endearingly   She was older than I had
curious, energetic and   pictured. That book-on-
perspicacious fellow we've   tape was not as new as I
all pledged our lives to.   had imagined. But she
My parents—well-meaning   was stunning,
but maddening in their   commanding all attention
loyalty to the Creationist   like a termite queen, or
creed—would have   an ovulating baboon.
preferred a different path
for their daughter, but
seeing as Darwin's father
believed his son would be
a disgrace to his family if
he continued his scientific
pursuits, at least I'm in
good company.

(Now, we begin to hear CRISTÓBAL *on the tape as well. In
order to recreate the moment, the live* CRISTÓBAL *will speak
the same lines as the* CRISTÓBAL *on the tape, so that it will
sound like* JANICE *is speaking with the live* CRISTÓBAL—*)*

JANICE: *(On tape)* So, in conclusion, I would like to
thank once again this august and illustrious body for
awarding me the Julian Huxley Medal for Outstanding
Darwinian Scholarship and it is my sincere hope that—

CRISTÓBAL: *(On tape, and live) Perdón,* excuse me! Excuse me, Miss Greene! *Señora!*

JANICE: *(On tape)* Uh yes, is there someone with a question?

CRISTÓBAL: *(On tape, and live)* I have been following your work for many years. I am Cristóbal!

JANICE: *(On tape. Bemused, though confused)* Okay—

CRISTÓBAL: *(On tape, and live)* I am a great fan!

JANICE: *(On tape)* Well thank you—

CRISTÓBAL: *(On tape, and live)* You sparkle like a night of stars witnessed from moonless Patagonian Plains!

JANICE: *(On tape)* Oh, well that's—

CRISTÓBAL: *(On tape, and live)* Yet you are many things—a puma's sharp claw, the terrible surf—sit down sir, I am talking!—you are these things Miss Greene, yet also those flowers of purple and yellow that just pop up on the roadsides in October—do you know of what I speak?

JANICE: *(On tape)* Uh, well I'm not quite sure—but if you have a question—

CRISTÓBAL: *(On tape, and live)* I am Cristóbal, sit down sir—you too!—or would you like more convincing from my blade!?—I am asking one question for the lady—If you may, Miss Greene—pardon my English, but I humbly ask…could you tell me please…where I can find Charles Darwin's Notebook of Sexual Conquests.

JANICE: *(On tape)* I beg your pardon?

CRISTÓBAL: *(On tape, and live)* I would like the list Charles Darwin compiled of all the ladies he has bedded.

JANICE: *(On tape)* I don't think—

CRISTÓBAL: *(On tape, and live)* You know—seduced. The list is long, no?

JANICE: *(On tape)* Um, if somebody could escort—

CRISTÓBAL: *(On tape, and live)* The museum where the list is housed!—that is all I need—

JANICE: *(On tape)* I believe this ceremony is over—

CRISTÓBAL: *(On tape, and live)* Get off me sirs! You are escorting me nowhere!

JANICE: *(On tape)* Um, thank you for coming, everyone—

CRISTÓBAL: *(On tape, and live)* I cannot leave until I— you think you are strong?!, well I— Aaah—my arm does not go like that! —Miss Greene! *Por favor!* I need your help! Janice!

(Pause. CRISTÓBAL *addresses the audience—)*

CRISTÓBAL: "Okay," I'm thinking. "To hell with Janice. For now." *(Brandishing "tree of life" scrap from bible)* No, a single scrap of unauthenticated Darwiniana is not going to attract a lady such as she. And thus…the crime spree alluded to in my Apology. For it became clear to me that, despite my illiteracy, I would have to become an archive unto myself.

With my stealth, my knack for camouflage, my speed, my nimbleness, and my handy-dandy knowledge of alarm systems, no repository of Darwin's detritus would be safe. I would scoop up anything that looked promising and sift through it later, side by side with Janice, seeking references to Darwin's dalliances in Tierra del Fuego. That was my plan. How did I get to these repositories? How did I know where to go? Is it true that a cuchillo can really disengage a lock, if slid between the door and door jamb of a renowned German collector? Did I really obtain all fourteen of Darwin's field notebooks? These questions of yours?—

they are stupid. I am Cristóbal *and I survive* because
I adapt. It is as Darwin said—those species survive
which are the Fittest.

You do understand, do you not, that survival of the
fittest does not mean survival of those who go most
often to the gym. Not *"physically* fit." Hanh? Picture
me, naked. I am…Where You Live. A coral reef, a
slimy pond, the stomach of a rhinoceros—it doesn't
matter, I am Environment, and I am naked. My legs
are this long, my buttocks protrude as so. My waist is
thus. You, sir, *(Points to a man in the audience)* are a pair
of pants. I will now try you on. No. You are no good.
You ride up my groin, you are uncomfortable, it is not
a good fit, I toss you aside. *(Points to another)* You—you
are a pair of pants. *(Points to others—)* And you and
you. You are all pants. You must think of species as
pants and you must think of the world as me. Naked.
One of you will fit me best and the others I will cast
aside. And the one of you that fits me best? I will order
twenty pairs. *That* is survival of the fittest. You see?
Ah— *But I—Environment—I may change.* Are you still
picturing me naked? Good. I get fat. The pants that
once fit no longer fit, damn it!—is there another pair of
pants?!, one that will fit me better?, no not you, or you,
how about you, are you going to pinch my waistline?,
you see?—can you hear it?— the engine of natural
selection is revving up again.

So. Now you can understand…that when I find myself
out in the world, *I thrive.* Despite the conditions.
Because I am a highly adjustable pair of pants. I'm like
sweats. Or Chinos—appropriate in many different
situations. Dockside parties. Bar Mitzvahs. Okay? You
get it? Look, English is my second language and even I
could have told Charles Robert "no, find a better word
than 'fittest'. You will be misunderstood."

Are you still picturing me naked? You may now stop if you wish. Or continue. I leave it to you.

So. I said, "Janice, I think this notebook here could be good, let's start with this one." She said, "who are you and how the hell did you get into my house." She put down her groceries. She was beautiful. Well-preserved. She wanted to call the police but hesitated when she saw my haul of contraband Darwin. Her jaw dropped and her eyes gleamed and I wanted to kiss her. It was annoying I was distracted in this way but what could I do?—I had the hot blood of Charles Darwin running through me and we Darwins are a lusty bunch.

She had no husband—divorced—and she waited too long to have children, so that house in Atlanta Georgia was empty save for me, her, and a whole lot of old paper. She still wanted to call the police but I showed her the Tree of Life that started my quest, and dove headlong into my tale before she could get a clear picture in her head of where she kept her pepper spray.

She knew Ushuaia. She spent a whole year researching there in the '60s, fresh out of school, a special time there in Tierra del Fuego, she said. "It is a special place", though clouds and sun both mixed on her face, as she said this. As if she knew what she discovered there would change her. As it did for Darwin. As it did for me. She didn't believe me about my Tree of Life. She figured I had nicked it with the rest of my plunder, and this gave me hope—it meant it belonged in the bunch!

So I asked her again—where is Darwin's Notebook of Sexual Conquests. She said, like a woman, that he doesn't have one. And she said there was a far more effective way to confirm a line between me and Old Man Darwin. *A Genetic Test.*

Hanh?

D N A. Darwin did not know about D N A, and boy I bet he wishes he had. The hair of a chimp, the hair of a man, a little labwork voodoo and you find ninety-nine percent of the genetic code is the same. In 1859? That would have helped.

But it could still help *me*! Give me the test and it'll show that I'm Darwin! "No," said Janice, you must also get a sample of Darwin's D N A.

Hanh? But he's dead.

"His descendants. The test would show a common paternity. But for an accurate reading you would have to scrape the inside of the cheek of one of Darwin's descendants with a long cotton "buccal" swab. So forget it."

(Holding up lock of hair) "What about my mother's hair!? I have a lock!"

"With hair, they can profile the mitochondrial D N A," she explained, "the D N A that is passed down woman to woman. All it would show is that she is your mother. A genetic portrait." *(Moved)* A portrait of who she is? Deep down? I want that. Send it in. And then? Make some calls—cause I'm not going back to Ushuaia without buccal swabbing a Darwin!

As luck would have it, there was a gathering of Darwins at his ancestral home in Kent. Drumming up publicity for a Wildflower Survey. Many scholars would be there. Janice didn't want to go. I said I would go on my own and seek out Erasmus Darwin. Erasmus was the name of Charles Darwin's grandfather, who put out a book on evolution before Charles was born. That Erasmus, of course, was dead. But Erasmus was *also* the name of Darwin's *great grandson*, now an elderly man. Being not as robust, he was one I could easily peel away from the herd of fleeing Darwins, and

overpower. I would jump him. And swab him. Janice
decided to go, to keep me out of trouble.

It was a nighttime function. A party. Lots of appetizers.
And scholars. I blended in. *(Pointing)* And there was
Sarah Darwin—a great great granddaughter, and there
was Chris Darwin—too burly for my purposes—and
little Allegra Darwin—I could probably take her but
toddlers were unpredictable—and then, *I saw my
quarry.* Erasmus. He had blue eyes. He was holding
a stuffed mushroom and a flute of champagne so his
hands were useless to defend himself. I waited for a
moment when Janice had to leave to use the Ladies'.
And as if a sign that this was indeed my Destiny, the
music now playing…*was tango.*

(We hear Tango Nuevo music as CRISTÓBAL *dramatically
unsheathes his buccal swab—it resembles a cotton swab with
a long stick)*

My buccal swab.

*(*CRISTÓBAL *approaches an unseen Erasmus as in a cross
between a dance and the approach of the picador in a
bullfight)*

The hubbub faded, the dance floor cleared, it was just
me and he, my cousin. Sure we're family, but young
pelicans push their own siblings out of the nest. That's
Nature brother. *So here I come.* Now all eyes were upon
me. Hypnotized, they followed my advance. And
then…a scream. It might have been Allegra but I think
it was Chris. The spell was broken. I jumped Erasmus
like a man possessed. His mouth had been agape for
the last five minutes so my job was easy—*fwoosh!*—I
swabbed him.

But there was then a ruckus. Get off me! And get off
my buccal swab! I could hear Janice shouting as if in a
dream, and though I got the hell out of there, my swab

fell to the floor. And all it would show me now is that I was related to dustmites, pillbugs, and maybe a mouse.

It was in all the tabloids, or so I hear—reporting that I was Janice's boy toy. But only because I shouted out that I was her boy toy. She was furious, but I followed her home to pick up my mother's profile now back from the lab. "No," she said, looking at the report. "You used the wrong hair." I didn't. "Then they mixed up the sample. The mutation for blue eyes is a single letter change, from A to G, on the long arm of chromosome 15. But look—" "A-A"—both strands. Hanh?! What are you saying?! "Your blue eyes means your mother should have a `G' here. This profile is tainted. I'm sorry, now get out."

I raged at her. The whole world was conspiring to deny me even a simple link to my past! I did *not* appear out of nothing! I stormed out and realized a week later I had forgotten my *cuchillo*—she had taken it from me when I first arrived and locked it in her desk drawer.

So I went back and found not her but two elderly thieves, clearing out her belongings. Out! Shoo! Or mark my words, this day will be your last! They were Janice's parents. Did I not read the newspapers? I explained I was not really her boyfriend. What? No. Hit and run? She is dead?

(Pause, then intensely)

Not everything proceeds in imperceptible increments…Darwin didn't get everything right. The history of Life is also punctuated with sudden calamity… Obliteration… A hit and Bloody run…

"She's alive in Christ now."

Hanh?

"Alive. In Christ."

Oh yeah, these were her famous fundamentalist folk—I
had forgotten. The ones who gave her a hell of a time
for envisioning a world a hundred million times older
than they envisioned it. I could have spit on them for
their ignorance, I am a champion spitter. But they were
in pain.

"There are four hundred thousand species of beetles," I
said to them. "That's a lot of beetles on a boat," and left
it at that.

I went up to Janice's room, jimmied open her desk,
took my cuchillo and, what the hell, took everything in
there. Cleaned her out. And, Eyes Burning, I decided
then and there to dare the most audacious and heroic
caper this world had ever witnessed!

Darwin, you see, had wished to be buried with quiet
dignity, in his local churchyard. And that's practically
what he got. They buried him in Westminster Abbey.
And now his great great great great grandbastard
wanted his D N A very badly. I was *done* playing
around! The little pinky toe of Charles Darwin would
be mine!

Such a heist would require a year of careful planning,
so I gave it a week, because I am Cristóbal. I blended
in with a Japanese tour group and determined I would
spend the hours between closing time and two A M
cloistered in the Norman Undercroft. *Crouching.*

My crotch went numb. It was uncomfortable. But
Darwin? After returning home on the Beagle, he
suffered the rest of his days with unexplained
malaise, vertigo, dizziness, tremors, vomiting, cramps,
headaches, and eczema. So I could put up with a numb
crotch.

And then it was time.

(The lights turn out, he turns on a flashlight.)

Padding down the silent empty nave. Past Isaac
Newton, William Pitt, Charles Dickens—my tour guide
told us who these people were. But it was in Japanese
so *(Shrugging ["the hell if I know"]—) pfff*. But I had kept
an ear pricked for "Charles Darwin" and here he was.
The slab would need prising, but tiles next to it were
loose, and with my bag of tools it was not difficult to
get at the lid—I slid it back…I'd have to work fast for
dawn was approaching and—….

…and there he was. Bones. His last book was on
worms you know. "I wanted to write about the worm
before I join them myself," he said. *(looking at unseen
corpse)* These are the bones of a homo sapien. I have
these bones. If you've lived, you have these bones.
The bones of this underachieving overachieving
bewildering little species. And we're all kin. We're all
kin. "Keep your damn toe. Grandfather." It was time
to go. Okay, the door is locked. This one too. And the
system is on. But not a problem—red wire, yellow wire
(Swinging cuchillo*) —fwoosh!*

(Ideally—we hear bells, alarms, and sirens)

Okay. Now it's a problem. And now, here I am, told to
apologize. "For desecrating a sacred monument, and
pilfering"….—no, the only thing I will apologize for is
making off with Janice's personal effects. That…that
was a transgression.

(He takes out a sealed envelope labeled "To Garth")

I can't even read them!

*(Suddenly realizing, and turning to a random woman in the
audience)*

But you can. Madam—I implore you—they are about
to take me back—what does this say?

RANDOM WOMAN IN AUDIENCE: *(Reading)* "To Garth."

CRISTÓBAL: Hanh? Who is Garth?! *(He rips open the letter and thrusts it at the* WOMAN.*)* Read! Read!

RANDOM WOMAN IN AUDIENCE: *(Reading)* For years I've wanted to tell you the truth. But who knows if I'll ever send this letter. Garth—you returned to Australia in November of '65, and it wasn't until December that I learned I was carrying your child. My parents are fundamentalists—they would have cast me out. I had no choice but to stay in Ushuaia, deliver your son, and let him go. But he's yours, make no mistake—down to his tiny webbed feet—yes, webbed! Just like yours! A genetic trait that seemed only to—

*(*CRISTÓBAL, *brain afire, has heard enough—he snatches the letter. In a daze, contemplating this revelation   )*

CRISTÓBAL: "Deliver your son...and let him go...in Ushuaia..."

*(*CRISTÓBAL *replays a passage of* JANICE *reading the final lines of Origin of the Species, now with music underscoring—)*

JANICE: "It is interesting to contemplate an entangled bank, clothed with many plants of many kinds, with birds singing on the bushes, and with worms crawling through the damp earth, and to reflect that these elaborately constructed forms, so different from each other and dependent on each other in so complex a manner, have all been produced by laws acting around us. There is grandeur in this view of life...that whilst this planet has gone cycling on according to the fixed law of gravity, from so simple a beginning endless forms most beautiful and most wonderful have been, and are being evolved."

(As we hear the above, after a few lines we hear over it the below, and the Darwin quote fades down...)

JANICE: *(Confidential, as in an audible whisper, intimate, with great maternal warmth)* Cristóbal, my dear one, now it is time. Do not let them keep you. Begin gathering your things for they are coming for you, and you do not have time for them. Hours are precious. Minutes are precious. Cup them in your hand for those droplets are your Life. Do I have to count to five? Go. Move.

CRISTÓBAL: *(Live. To recording, a little lost)* Where do I go?

(By the middle of the below, CRISTÓBAL has exited.)

JANICE: *(Gently answering)* Go to Australia. Your father is there. Your father is there, and who knows? In 1836, the H M S *Beagle*, with Charles Darwin aboard, landed in Australia for a two-month stay. Darwin mingled with both the natives and the immigrants. Perhaps did *more* than mingle. For I have no idea, no idea at all, who bequeathed to Garth—who handed down to your father—his sparkling, his mysterious and confoundingly deep…blue…blue…eyes.

END OF PLAY

Appendix A: The Full Text of Janice's Letter to Garth

July 18, 1971

For years I've wanted to tell you the truth. But who knows if I'll ever send this letter. Garth—you returned to Australia in November of '65, and it wasn't until December that I learned I was carrying your child. My parents are fundamentalists—they would have cast me out. I had no choice but to stay in Ushuaia, deliver your son, and let him go. But he's yours, make no mistake—down to his tiny webbed feet—yes, webbed! Just like yours! A genetic trait that seemed only to mock my predicament—a young Darwin scholar who had fallen for a fellow scholar and conducted her own inadvertent experiments in Mendelian heredity. Ugh, listen to me—it's no wonder it ended badly between us.

He's turning five next month. And there hasn't been a day, an hour, in these five years that I haven't thought of him. Not a single day. But it's too late. Life cycles on and it's too late for regrets. I don't even know his name. He's gone. But he lives. He lives, and I wanted you to know.

I will always love you.

Janice

Appendix B: P A Announcement

The Federal Bureau of Prisons, under the auspices of the United States Department of Justice, would like to extend their gratitude to those in attendance this [evening/afternoon]. Since authorized in the second session of the 110th Congress, the Felon Rehabilitation Through Public Repentance Program has proven to be a humane and effective tool in preparing carefully selected prisoners for their eventual return to society. The absence of security guards notwithstanding, the risks have been minimized—the prisoner has been chosen for his docility and willingness to cooperate. However, by remaining in your seats, you are understood to have waived your right to litigate should unforeseen events transpire. To lower the risk of prisoner aggression, we recommend taking this opportunity to turn off your cell phones. Also, please do not feed the prisoner—his diet is carefully regulated. Feeding Times with Demonstration are posted in your program. Thank you again and enjoy the Apology.

Appendix C: Darwin's "Tree of Life" from his Transmutation Notebook B

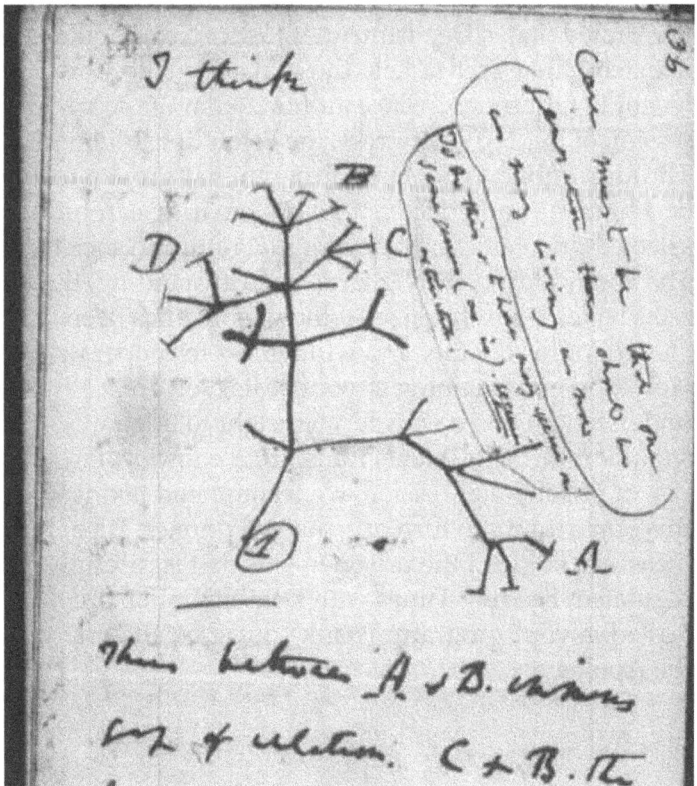